Time Transcendence
Expansion: Budding Seeds

Andre O Doeman

Time Transcendence
Expansion: Budding Seeds

River of Streams Publishing

Time Transcendence
Expansion: Budding Seeds

Copyright © 2025 by Andre O Doeman

River of Streams Publishing

All rights reserved. No part of this publication may be reproduced, distributed, or transmitted in any form or by any means, including photocopying, recording, digital scanning, or other electronic or mechanical methods, without the prior permission of the publisher. For permission requests or information, please address River of Streams Publishing at rstreamspublishing@gmail.com
Telephone: 718-717-3464

ISBN: 978-1-7362378-9-2

Cover Designs/ Illustrations by Andre O Doeman

Dedication

To Ash's becoming like the Sun rising

To Teeks for listening like the soothing Ocean

To Lexi, my little teacher like the Earth which refuses to falter.

Acknowledgements

Ever since quotations caught my attention, I began my own creation of them. Each of these poem titles are like little quotations with a deeper message in the poems themselves. As my writing developed, the encouragement and support over the years led to my completion of this book and for that, I thank you all.

To my mother for always teaching that "manners takes you through the world." That lesson was reinforced with clarity a few years ago. It was a remind to just be kind, be patient, and life will give you what you give to it. Keep on being relentless in your pursuits mother.

To my father, who always said the following lines to my sisters and I as a child in patois, "nothing name 'can't" and "read a book" for every response to the sign of 'giving up.' As a result, his own values have made him the most hardworking and relaxed person I have ever known. I still live by those words too, father.

Persephone, the lengthwise conversations about wealth, health, spiritual growth, and so many other ideas were invaluable as well as the feedback on how to improve one's self. I truly appreciate your reminding me of what it means to stand strong in one's aura and always giving feedback on my poems.

Fatima, one of the most instrumental women in my growth. Thank you for listening to my thoughts and my jokes all the time, daily, when I came to your office. Your impartial advice, encouragements, and understanding gave me strength.

Dr. Barnaby, your pivotal advice and presence during times of need gave me the strength to carry on. From conversations about growth, awareness to understanding, and transformation, you gave valuable insight into how I shaped the experiences within these works of poetry.

Gabe and Bryan, for the continued encouragement and support in my journeys and endeavors up to the writing of this book. Along with the MILES group and the extensive conversations about becoming men, the growth has been invaluable and one that has contributed to a few of the poems in this book. Thank you both.

Maria, I remember the final question in the African Diaspora class, "how do you want to be identified" – by skin complexion, ethnic group, or nationality among other identifiers. That question is one I still grapple with today, but it has also made me reflect on word origins continually.

Dr. Drake, for shifting my dislike of classical writing. Chaucer's "Canterbury Tales" was the beginning of my understanding of language's power and evolution. Nowadays, sonnets are at times beautiful and appealing.

Dr. Doggett, for teaching in such a way that made me recognize how much I needed to do to gain a better understanding of the ways to apply the written and spoken word. Without those tools, this book would not have been materialized.

Dr. McCoy, to this day, a lot of the ways I use language has been heavily influenced by your teaching techniques. Thank you for being a guide to the entrance of what it means to truly 'feel' and 'see' the important moments when I felt like I was losing grip on the ideas in my mind.

Mr. Q, thank you for the constant motivations and reminders of community and standing within your purpose and gifts. Without community, this next level wouldn't have been achieved.

To the rest of my family and friends who recognized the depths I would go to in conversation, who listened and reciprocated with understanding, who continued to give encouragement and insight, I thank you all very much. The experiences and interactions with you have contributed greatly to the developing and completion of this book.

Preface

"To love is to recognize yourself in another" Eckhart Tolle.

You are me and I am you. We are you and you are us.

When I began my teacher preparatory program, one of the required assignments my teachers and supervisors within the program emphasized was the need to journal daily and often with a reflective mindset. Today, I still do it whether it is writing, talking to myself, meditating through sitting still and thinking, or drawing what's on my mind. All of it led to my finding a solution to whatever problem I may have been facing which continues to work today both in poetic and artistic reflection.

Reflecting requires both a looking back and a looking forward. The in-between is the act in the present that helps you understand the past and embrace the future. Before and during the creation of this book, both this version and the previous version, I looked back on the afflictions of my college peers and the young people and adults of today. I also think about what the future may entail for them if they begin reflective practice daily with discipline. Consequently, they may come to understand it as not as a quick process to check off, but a requirement for one's self-development through painstaking effort in mental work and patience to find a solution. Ultimately, this benefits the individual who will realize the possible troubles they face or have been facing, the dissociation they may have tried which may have led to an attempted stifling of pain (a running from what will continue to follow), and the importance of and value in facing life's troubles no matter how much pain is felt.

In the early 2000's, for many, attending therapy was becoming more prevalent and by the decade, perhaps at the beginning of 2013 and onward, depression and anxiety, two of the most cited mental health disorders, became more widespread in conjunction with the fast development of technology and social media that bombards people with images and language that paradoxically asserts self-love at its core. It also emphasized implicitly the need for one to change their entire physique and mind to be able to love themselves adequately. As an educator, I have seen its impact mostly on adolescents who are in an extreme period of mental, physical, and emotional development. Their belief in their own invincibility, an ego that heightens their self-importance, and a focus only on the here and now, prevents them from even attempting to do reflective practice. It is in that instance where the problem lies. To change one's being without reflection and consideration is to disregard the consequences of one's action that can be life impacting for a very long time. Adolescence, but even more so, many adults of today, are still dealing with life impacting decisions that they made which affects the generation that many continue to the label with the maxim "Children are the Future." We must remember that a decision that has the backing of foresight to see its potential impact, no matter how slow or fast the decision was, is more valuable than an impulsive one.

When it comes to the children who we say are the future, whatever decisions we make as it relates to them becomes even more significant. I was once a child of the future. You were one too. Regardless of maturity, we are raising the new ones of the future. And we cannot do it without reflecting on how we can do it and what we must work on individually to help the children who will also be beneficial in helping the community's growth. The community becoming better thrives on empathy, an act that requires listening, thinking, reflecting, and attempting to take on another person's feelings to understand their perspective respectfully. Children raising children is not as conducive to invaluable outcomes as compared to mature adults raising children as a village and a community. While that is an obvious conclusion, one only need to take a look at the media that is raising our young people.

To be mature and responsible means that no matter the decision you made, no matter how undesired the consequences are, you understand that you have a commitment and principle to hold on to and carry out. Part of that is ensuring that "each one teaches one"; it is ensuring that we raise our youth as a community reflectively; it means that we discern members of the village and their intentions respectfully while abiding by principle. It means that we hold each other accountable and responsible for the duty we must carry out so that our youth learn to reflectively face their problems head-on; so that they fall down and learn while they are on the ground, so that they can rise like a phoenix again. And as we carry out our duties and commitments, we stand on the sidelines as a guide pushing the youth forward. This is the collective awakening of a community, a village, and it can only happen with patience, time, and reflective action of the mind.

Major Themes and the Importance of Balance

Life is a journey and a cycle of check points wherein one stops, reflect on their learning thus far, and decides on the next course of action to take for attaining the next level of growth. This is the purpose of the, *Time Transcendence Series*. Undoubtedly, this journey is not possible by one's own actions alone. The journey requires the input of others and one's discernment in a variety of ways. Those before us are like the trees within the forest of mother nature. We are the little plants looking up and receiving guidance in the form of pollen to help us grow through the journey.

Trees and plants are among the major themes in this book of poetry. We need them for life, the air we breathe, the herbs and medicines we consume, among other things. But trees are also a symbol of wealth, life, and mental strength. The adinkra symbols of the Akan people of Ghana conveys proverbs and wisdom about life. Similarly, other objects of the world and universe along with animals are also symbolic within the poems and the art. Colors, as symbols, also play important roles in understanding the poems, the images, as well as the context of the poems. All the symbols may represent either side of a coin, yin and yang. The truth of the matter is that life must not be lived with the intention that it will always be only joy and happiness. We are humans after all, and we will always experience negative emotions as much as we experience positive ones. We all want to remain in the positive aspects of our emotions, but we must remember that the negative ones are needed. This is neither good nor bad. It is just balance. When we feel one thing, somehow, if it is too much, our minds often want to tip the scale back to the middle.

Imagine the sadness we feel to see a malnourished starving child. It compels us to help to ensure nourishment to that child. Anger compels us to act without thought and even that is a balancing act. To feel is to act to become. On the other hand, think of the relationships between people. Sometimes, a moment may be going extremely well, and one person decides to ask a question or make a comment about a random situation or thought. The other person might wonder at its relevance, or it may compel the person to search for answers which can lead them to a path that is more problematic.

The best thing about this is that it is understood. This is often the case when a person reflects on the rationality of it all. If you are a person who is often a disciple of the heart, actions led by thought may not make sense sometimes and vice versa. The important thing to do here is understand the process by which a person takes their journey. As mentioned, it is neither bad nor good, but rather, it is needed. This is the yin and yang of our world. Which one are you? To get to that answer, you must reflect, and you must do so with the village and the community.

I continue to think about balance and my changing views over the last decade through my continual reflection of being and what it means to be, my recognition of the spectrums of being, and being in balance within ourselves, with each other, with the village we want to build for generations to come, and with the maturing of the world. *We Are The World* as the famous song written by Michael Jackson and Lionel Richie emphasized. Our spirits between each other are thinly and invisibly connected. This is not something that can be seen, it is the flow of energy to be felt just through the recognition that you are the world, and everyone is a part of you trying to build the world as we practice the act of balance through reflection for action. This practice to build arrives within us as a sense of purpose and a realization that there is something greater than ourselves individually. That thing, that entity, that spirit, or whatever you wish to call it is our calling to be better for ourselves and each other.

Thank you for obtaining *Time Transcendence: Expansion: Budding Seeds*. I hope, throughout and by the end of this book and the subsequence ones, you will understand the power of reflective practice and action toward a collective awakening.

Purpose of Activities: "Budding Seeds."

"Budding Seeds" is about caring for oneself. With some help from someone else, it must allow one to get to a place of deep awareness in and of their development that impacts other people. More importantly, keep pushing forward to build your purpose regardless of the hate that will come. The activities serve for this purpose as well as a compelling force for one to understand the beginning of things, the innocence of being a child in a world that at once appears as innocent too. The questions and activities are about growth and thought. Essentially, take care of oneself in order to be able to take care of others; this leads us to an awakening in time collectively.

Table of Contents

Part 1 Budding Seeds 12
Earth's Birth 13
Soul's Journey: Two Folds. 18
God of Medicine (c. 2980 B.C.) 22
Baby in a Cocoon 26
Shadow and Moon 31
Lite an Wata 36
King's Chapel 40
Wine Glasses 44
Creature's Kiss 49
Danger Beyond The Ring 53
Mother's Love 57
Memory 62
The Ablest Queen (c. 1500 B.C.) 67
Animal Love 72
Foreign Mi Guh 76
Sculpted Years: Yaad Memories 81

Part 1

A child enters the world loving everything as it explores. As that child becomes, the world shows that child that hate will be along the road of exploration. Nonetheless, the child keeps moving forward.

Budding Seeds

Earth's Birth

The origin of all of nature's things is the mother, thus, remember to give back thankfully.

Spherical, bluish marble,
cracks of grassy giants,
brown earth
with paints of umber dirt.
Mother nature's leafy coverings
atmospheric blankets hovering,
cradling oxygen for beings soon to exist
along with other necessary gases; nitrogen, *carbon*-O2
pours into *plants holding hands* with the spirits of *Olu*
as a bridge for bonds long overdue.

With the help of the heated ball in the sky
chilling with a system of planets and stars
living, the reason for inhabitants'
existence certainly, may *WE* transform a dust ball
into a blooming orb, a better participant.
Breeze blows on by cutting through
     falling
          water -
               falls, and rising [rivers,]
muddy palms to rugged hands,
bound by the flourishing
marble to be and all in between.
May we unearth
by living, digging
through mortality's dirt

like creators diving for meanings
in the deep. Flutter kicking
below, then floating ashore

capturing a ball of energy in *fours*,
grasping the   *fire*   that soars,
     igniting freedom's flames with
       fresh   *air*   blowing a twirl of   *dirt.*
Liquid   solidifying,
cells multiplying
to shape *US*.

Organisms,
start the engines of your minds
to drive cells,
continue to multiply.

1) **Reflection Actions**
   a. **Transformative Journey – Mother Earth and You**
      i. What does "connecting" to Mother Earth/ nature mean to you? List a few ways we can show gratitude to the Earth
      ii. What does transformation mean in your life? Share an example of a personal transformation you've experienced

2) **Creative Activities**
   a. **Nature Collage:**
      i. Create a collage using images from magazines or drawings that represent different elements of nature described in the poem (e.g., plants, water, earth).

   b. **Planting a plant: Air Exchanges**
      i. The snake plant is known as a natural air purifier. This is a good plant to have. If you have another plant, that is fine as well. Be sure to water your plant and provide sunlight to it daily. Take care of it as you take care of yourself.

3) **Group Discussion (if applicable)**
   a. What role do you play in forming and taking care of the Earth/ environment?
   b. How can we balance our needs while ensuring the health of Mother Earth?

Soul's Journey: Two Folds.
The soul thrives when you ensure to take care of your physical reality of you and others

Dancing forests of Souls,
    blossoming red roses,
the toddler saplings of old,
    Mother Nature, as a musician composes

    a bird's flight to the heavens,
off our Earthly soles,
    with twelves and sevens
beyond the clear sky is the goal

    bridges build themselves between
where transformation unfolds,
    a sparkling sight to see
as their journey molds...

    they vine upward; little sunshine plants
before the age they bloom out of the home
    as Earth revolves; budding, then supplants
to climb upward once again. As if lost, they roam

    long after flourishing seedlings
while consuming stories of roses unfolding
    to hike the **Third Star** *while delving*
in journeys of rebirths of the soul.

1) **Reflection Actions**
    1. **Connections to the Soul – The Outer and The Inner**
        i. What do you believe could be the **Third Star** as you think about the lines in the poem?
        ii. How might the poem zig-zag form relate to the soul's journey?
2) **Creative Activities**
    1. **Symbols of Life**
        i. As you consider what the "**Third Star**" could mean to you as well as your own journey in life thus far, create a symbol that represents you in whatever format you would like.
    2. **Letter to Young You**
        i. Write a letter to "the you" before you were born. Discuss all that you are experiencing before you come into the world.
        ii. Put the letter away. Re-read it after this book and each of the next books and reflect on it..
3) **Group Discussion (if applicable)**
    1. What does the "soul's journey" mean to you? What does it look like as the soul journeys through the world?
    2. How can we support each other's journeys in our community?

God of Medicine (c. 2980 B.C.)
The Earth is the medicine for your body caring for and building your soul; After all, it is you in a different form.

Herbs, with opened leaves
handed to me their elixirs of vitality
veining through their vines.
My thank you's rolled off my tongue
like an   air-filled   orb with CO_2 hugs
in exchange for the med. lessons they gave
me as a young, *golden*
mahogany Prince to cure all.

My wisdom, an owl, froze
Horus', Zeus', Jupiter's
mind, gluing them in a web of discoveries,
like the peace of a calm lake I sewed
into bodies before they
fell
       into
       graves.

Eastern Wood Pewees sing with the *Citrils*
in the early mornings
as you rest your eyes to relax
in your reforming.
It is a wonderful tune to drink
to quench your stress to think
and supply food to your mind.
They deified me as Imhotep,
the *Peace* of time.

1) **Reflection Actions**
    a. **Earth is Thy Medicine – Wisdom in History**
        i. Consider how the medicine you have taken throughout your life have impacted your vitality. What changes, if any, would you make regarding the medicines you consume?
2) **Creative Activities**
    a. **Meditative Mind**
        i. Take a nature walk after reading the poem and pay attention to how you sensing all things of nature around you. Illustrate what you sensed the most.
            1. (you may play some meditative/ peaceful instrumentals at a low volume)
        ii. Close your eyes and meditate on what a conversation of gratitude would be between you and a herb/ plant of your choosing. Illustrate that conversation in whatever format you choose.

3) **Group Discussion (if applicable)**
    a. How can we integrate natural remedies or practices into modern medicine?
    b. How do historical figures, our families, and history itself affect how we heal daily?

Baby in a Cocoon
Children are the future of today; be the lighthouse of guidance.

Forests' blissful singing mixed with angry shouts
~~spear through belly skins~~
of *cocoon's* translucency.
Letters formed into language,
blends of *rainbow*s, both *salad* and *mud,* and *in-betweens*.

Love?
    a ball of cloud caressing the rain inside,
    a cushion drinking warm touches from all sides,
    touches relaying the rays it receives from the sky
    then it reaches with its hovering and gives to all
    …a life.

Pain and Fear?
    the *Sheathed Swords* of the world,
    inconspicuous, never heard,
    wait to scythe babies in curls.
    There they lay in the dark, a glisten without care
    for babies whom drink love more than fear.
    For others, a *swift sword* slashes and tears
    a baby's heart, molding mortals' *spears*.

Joy?
    a gift longing to be opened with tiny hands
    glazed over by shiny eyes,
    carved on smile
    inspired by a choir of *Robins* in harmony,
    followed by *Blackbirds'* melodies
    in spring mornings. A symphony

paints existence on teeming globes:
beams of rays peeking through ocean-like skies
continue to bake emerald forests rich in wealth.

A zest filled star in its freshness says 'bye' then 'hi'
to the sun's ascension above heavy, puffy vapors
as roosters crow to the universe aloud with
a glee of optimism for life.

The babies' gaze glues onto *Blue Birds'* carols
matching the tempo of oceans' splashing.
Lightning zig zags its way across the sky
on a journey as its tail disappears swiftly;
the blink of an eye follows babies' '*goo gah*' quickly.

Babies' legs prepare to stand on stages innocently,
unknown to the world, they grin with certainty
ready to be
with what they guzzled in heaps
while growing in a cocoon.

1) **Reflection Actions**
    i. **Conversation with Mother Nature**
        1. Talk to a young child and ask him/her about their day, their hopes, their dreams. Be an encouraging ear like someone may have been for you. Remind the young child of the importance in being a light for others too. Write about it or draw your learning.

2) **Creative Activities**
    i. **Protective Shell**
        1. Today, take one to three actions that you are afraid of doing. Think about your process first and then make it happen. After you take the action/s, reflect and journal on the lines below, how you felt before and after doing the action/s.
    ii. **Drawing the Song**
        1. Get a pencil, and turn on your favorite song.
        2. Draw all that comes to mind for the entire song however you wish
        3. Once finished, look at the art you produced and ask yourself how it gives you a positive outlook on life.
        4. Consider if that song should remain in your life or not and possibly change it for the better

3) **Group Discussion (if applicable)**
    i. Can a baby truly be influenced by the sounds of the world while it is in its mother's womb? How so?
    ii. Why might pain, fear, love, and joy be together in the poem?

Shadow and Moon
Follow the moon, for it will never put you on the wrong path

Mother, the moon, the silver orb
subtly frolicked in the night sky
dipping behind stars toward me
like an annoying guardian, pursued me
to sprinkle its silver light over me
which emanated an aura of inspiration to lead the way
for others who might have lost their own way.
Despite my clamors with flailing arms,
it smiled at me as if to comprehend
the logic of my shouts
of my silent heart crying out.

If it stopped trailing me,
maybe I would be the crying boy
whose father   strolled,   then trudged away.
Or like those who were left with a
                                  cliff-hanger
in their favorite novel,
or like those who never got a conclusion
for the relationship's story
or like those who ate, with bloated eyes,
confusing combinations of words in conversations
which left their thoughts in a tangle,
trying to untangle
to find a closure.
The moon never allowed me to absorb those ways.
It was there like a cradling basket.

If my snorts froze it in the sky,
the stars were loyal guardian
angels, guards on duty,
ready to intervene just in case
my path veered off course.
My shadow, who committed
more religiously than the moon
was a ninja in the night
preparing for a battle and a fight
with guidance from the moon
in guiding me too.

Slowly,
my nights began to brightened with
glows of a decorated galaxy of vitality
as *Shadow* escorted me;
it was time to watch over me
from below
like a guardian angel
I appreciated but did not know.

During slumber,
Shadows hopped onto the moon
for they had a duty to attend to
for many little ones on planet blue
hoping to have a friend too
in shadow and moon.

1) **Reflection Actions**
    i. **Eye Contest with a Guardian**
        1. As you think about the moon and its interconnection with the sun, how do you practice balance in your life with the things you enjoy and the people around you?
        2. How are you a guardian to your soul and to someone else?

2) **Creative Activities**
    i. **Moon Essence Reflection**
        1. Create a story-web with you in the center in the form (a shape) of your choice.
        2. Create the outer aspects of the web with five people who have influenced or impacted you in accomplishing your goals. Choose their form.
        3. Write one word that connects you to them.
        4. Reach out to those people as often as you can with appreciation.

3) **Group Discussion (if applicable)**
    i. What symbols represent who you are as a person in the past, in your present, and possibly in your future?
    ii. Why might symbols be valuable to our growth and even to history itself?

Lite an Wata
With each other, we can have light and water.

Lite,
widout extra payment
nay joke fi guh weh,
an grandparents' brain did kno seh
cangle an kersin ile was deh ting fi get.
In a dem time deh,
darkness call out fi duppy stories weh
ave roots in a histery but sum seh
deh story dem did deh lie.
Anansi cool,
but *tree fut h-arse* did put
fear inna wi more wile.

Wata
free ting
nay joke fi guh weh,
gone from deh dry pipe dem.
Dem outta orda like deh
wata company dem.
Bac in a dem deh day,
fun was a all day ting
wen we bade dung a riva deh.
Rain wata in a wi pan pon deh step,
drum pon deh roof top
did full up a wata mi seh.

1) **Reflection Actions**
    i. **Be Light and Water My Friend**
        1. How are you being a light to others and water to yourself?
        2. What does "rain" itself mean to you as you think about this poem and the title of this book "Budding Seeds"?

2) **Creative Activities**
    i. **Light Tunes and Water Power**
        1. Create a playlist of your favorite songs if you do not have one and listen to at least three of those songs think about how the song's words differ from it's frequency and beat.
        2. Research an easy to do science experiment with water and pay attention to how the water moves in connection to its impact on our daily life.

3) **Group Discussion (if applicable)**
    i. If we did not have the sun in the sky, or if the sun was smaller/bigger than what we are told, how do you think our lives would be different? Explain.
    ii. Considering the poem, what are your thoughts on water being controlled by others?

King's Chapel
Believe in something greater than yourself as your vision becomes more achievable.

Deh voices dem bawl out to deh heavens
wen peeple andem lik up inna each ada.
Peeple fut did deh tep pon deh grung
wid confidence.
It luk like seh a deh adulation sumtime.

Likkle mind like mine
ardly pay attention to nuh a deh sines
wen talk wid joy pon one an,
and fury pon deh ada.

Suits an embellish dresses
luk like dem capcho the show every Sundeh mawnin'
more than the voices and praises.

King's Chapel dough,
the loudest mi eva guh to.
Mi sure seh the almighty heard deh requests
dem fi a **world a beauty**
mor dan the **tank you's** dem,
but memba seh,
a tank ful hart
will ave more art
on a canvas illustratin'
a beautiful world in duty.

1) **Reflection Actions**
   i. **Daily Gratitude of The Heart**
      1. Show appreciation to a higher power or the world around you in any way you wish.

2) **Creative Activities**
   i. **A Mantra**
      1. Find three quotes from any book at random.
      2. Create a story of light and positivity with those quotes
      3. Speak them out loud daily and speak to yourself as you look in your mirror.

   ii. **Home of Hearts**
      1. Draw what home means to you. As you draw, keep in mind words such as "village", "foundation", "rest", "appreciation."

3) **Group Discussion (if applicable)**
   i. What does the following quote mean to you, "it takes a village to raise a child?"
   ii. Do you believe our culture today is still upholding those words? Why or why not? What can be done?

Wine Glasses
Guard the youth; but do not deny them the truth.

My mind grappled with holding the question of
how two glistening **wine glasses**
across from each other,
which copper hands delicately grasped
and unsoiled lips sweetly sipped,
d e c o n s t r u c t e d
into
b r o k e n   p i e c e s laying on the ground
reddening the white tiles all around.
They were gentle like water
caressing the belief in my mind:
"soft, flowing, and *coupled* beings,
could never be b r o k e n."

On a birthday one day,
the sun forced my eyes open
removing my blinds,
indicating my joy in the birds' tunes,
but I blinked at a point as a child
and the night motioned, an opportunity
to drink my summer light
to regurgitate rain, washing away
all the light from my sight.
The tears
made my tongue twist with disgust,
like terrible medicine
that drew temporary marks on my face.
I began to resent
b r o k e n wine glasses.

A belief in "two loving beings"
remodeled into a mural of memories
painted in my teary eyes.

Tear

        drops

embodied drops of naivety
of a world of "wine glasses"
that kept shattering across the floor
hurting the rest of the house and more.
One time, puppy dog eyes appeared,
I was sent to get a band-aid near,
"sticking plaster",
the thunderous voice bellowed fear.

I just wanted to be in
between
"two loving beings"
rather than
b r o k e n
wine glasses,
but my tears cutting that possibility,
advised against it
because of a building of my scars of agony.

1) **Reflection Actions**
    i. **Truth in Hidden Gems**
        1. Reflect on any resentment or fears you have through writing or drawing as a way to challenge it.
        2. What experiences, if any, have you had in your life that has cracked you and forced you to put yourself back together with a lesson?

2) **Creative Activities**
    i. **Put it Together**
        1. Gather ten random items in your home (it could be anything at all), glue/ tape, and obtain a paper or canvas of any size you wish.
        2. Assign names/ symbols to the items to build their value
        3. As fast and as intentionally as you can, put all the items together in any way that comes to your mind on the paper/ canvas and tape/ glue them together.
        4. Once you are finished, admire with appreciation and put it some place you can look at any time when you feel life is testing your strength.

3) **Group Discussion (if applicable)**
    i. What reasons are there to protect a child from the evils of the world?
    ii. Is it reasonable to protect a child from the world, or does this go beyond the limitations of the question?

Creature's Kiss

Sometimes, life happens and it's up to you to walk and figure it out.

The buzzing sound lured Him into the room.
Curious eyes glued their attention to white curtains.
There the critter stood, chilling, unbothered.
His hand reached for a broom, but the
nimble Creature flew after the hand sign.
Lightning fast, His hand swung
but lady luck sprung
for the Creature who flew off the wall
refusing to die or fall.
It was like a mouse in a wary state,
like a stubborn kid, relaxed, defying fate.

Between the two, the shoe filled space on the floor
made our human mind map a plan with abhor.
"Tonight, one of those shoes will smack you to the floor
with a deafening roar."
Slowly, stealthily, like a panther moving toward its prey,
He swung and sharply missed even though he prayed.
Now, Creature the critter knew our human's intentions
were crystal clear.
So, it pitched lightly
as our human's eyes squinted, blindly
as Creature smiled wisely
upon the human's lips
for a swift second,
seemingly a dis'.
With a furious hand He brushed Creature rapidly
from there, and rushed swiftly
to the bathroom near.

1) **Reflection Actions**
    i. **Critters of Nature's Soul**
        1. The creature in this poem symbolizes either getting rid of negativity or adaptability, while the one in the image symbolizes protection and new beginnings. If you had to choose to be one of any living creatures in the world to be your partner in learning how to grow in life, which would you choose? Why?

2) **Creative Activities**
    i. **Creating The Creature**
        1. Draw your interpretation of what the creature is it looks like. You may color it however you wish.

    ii. **Meditate on It**
        1. Considering what the creature symbolizes; meditate for five minutes.
        2. With eyes close, envision your journey of the past, present, and future.
        3. As you meditate, pay attention to the checkpoints in your journey and how they have influence your present and will influence your future.

3) **Group Discussion (if applicable)**
    i. What does abundance and prosperity look like for you?

Danger Beyond The Ring

Teach the youth beyond dependence; that is the world's requirement.

"Blue Gums" were blue.
Shaded by the brush in pink and purple too,
with teeth reflecting the stains from candy
which they wanted to

remove.

But it was a fight with their toothbrush
with toothpaste mixed with red dripping out of their mouths
like the blood of painful carnage in the mind
pointing back to historical times.

The campaigns of today preach:
"tell someone, ask for help, it will be okay,"

failing to realize that Blue Gums can't defend themselves
when a diamond fortress covers them from a
dangerous reality.

Now, on their block, 7, 12, or 13 minutes from a

safe space,

enemies' eyes drool with desires of a debacle
and their anger misplaced
became for them, a successful case.

Now in a ring of fire, Blue Gums
now ask themselves one question,
"What skills did you give me family
to use beyond a diamond reality?"

1) **Reflection Actions**
   i. **Dependence within a Bubble**
      1. Look back at the poem "Baby in a Cocoon" and ask yourself, are you truly out of your cocoon or do you still sit in it with dependence? Whether you are out of it or not, write what you intend to do next in three steps.

2) **Creative Activities**
   i. **Symbol of Bravery and Protection**
      1. The image for this poem is represented by royal/ceremonial swords protecting a diamond. The swords are an adinkra symbol called "Akofena" which means bravery and valor. Draw what a safe space looks like as well as a symbol in your life that represents bravery and protection of that safe space.

3) **Group Discussion (if applicable)**
   i. Is Bullying a necessary evil? Why or why not?
   ii. What is a safe space? Is it truly needed?

Mother's Love

Be as committed as mother nature's roots which are tethered to its grasses all around

The water from mother's eyes
ran down her cheek
as her little ones took flight to the skies.
Her eyes
held onto footprints and streaks.
In her sky,
where her heart resided,
they never flew away,
fledglings, not ready for the day.

Nostalgia ate her psyche,
her memories iced,
froze her mind, prevented agitation,
but due to starvation
...
...
she jumped off her branch of opportunity,
hoping to birth bridge-like wings to reach them too.

When her hands finally grasped them,
like an apparent victory in tug-of-war
through a closing of the distance

       between them and her, incoming eclipse,

she realized her reach was insufficient
beyond her imagination,
beyond fruitful visions of hers.

Mother nature grew heated with hate at its insufficiency:
twisting winds, vibrating rocks, whirlpool gusting with breeze
wishing to produce a balance to human deficiencies.

But for her, our blue marble catered;
her love *sprung* while her hate *fell,*
her chi held on to mother nature
which never gave birth to a will to give up.
She was like a determined tree shooting up
because her relentlessness,
like the cuckooing climbs of the sun,
sent little bulbs packed of love
no matter the distance with
her memories, keeping up the run.

Mother's number one lesson:
"manners take you through the world"
and her survival to fly with her little ones
was her ensuring their manners
in time, like a flower, would certainly unfurl.

1) **Reflection Actions**
   i. **Flowerful Gratitude with Love**
      1. Reach out to three people who has given you the love of a mother and thank them person for always caring or, illustrate an image of love and gratitude to the world and give it to someone at random.

2) **Creative Activities**
   i. **Love and Foundation**
      1. Thinking about the importance of love and foundation for children, take ten minutes to draw what you think it looks like.

   ii. **Love symbol**
      1. In the image for this poem, the mother is wearing clips with a turtle on them – a symbol of resilience, creation, wisdom, and protection – all aspects of love. Draw a symbol that represents one of the words the turtle symbolizes.

3) **Group Discussion (if applicable)**
   i. What would you do if you had to let your child faced the world even if you felt like they weren't ready at all?
   ii. Is mother nature effective in raising children today as in the past? Is it better or worse?

Memory

Memory is a life of experiences that is worth building together for those to come.

Mother always said "writing reinforces memory"
and to this day, pens and pencils between my fingers
walk with the memory of those words in exploration
freely
after my people in *1962,*
as my *2000* BC pen
jot
into original
key   board   taps.
1864 tapped these memories
in the world of technology,
where typing suppresses
pencil on paper fervently.

Square formulas and *Canterbury Tales*
required toiling with letters and shapes,
while   *heliocentric theory*   held the championship flag
in *1610* as it revolved around our **Sunny** minds
in *religious* times.
History continues to remind
while forgetting better was before the *1400's.*

C. *2980 BC* welcomed the ***Prince of Peace,***
and *Timbuktu* put on display great geniuses
along with *The Congo's riches*
in remarkable numbers with *African Fractals*
full of illustrative designs
like stars mirroring shrines.

In *1569,* Maps lied so well on a country's size,
along with vertical and horizontal lines
with **Lat** and **Long** locations that tried it,
showing the east, west, the Equator,

and the *Prime Meridian* origins didn't mind it.

Now as I spit these words,
your world curls
back into its shell
to curate and unfurl
memory's shiny pearls
through today's keyboarding swirls.

A future of memories, what does it hold from a child whose brush battles reinforcing the paint from before?

1) **Reflection Actions**
    i. **Power of the Pen**
        1. How has one historical happening you have learned about impacted your perspective on life? What has been the advantages and disadvantages of the information age?

2) **Creative Activities**
    i. **Memories from Music**
        1. Consider the release date of ten of any song that you like.
            a. Create a poetic line for each of the songs (a theme and the song's year)
            b. Challenge yourself and memorize those ten lines
            c. Challenge: Recite and Perform it – to yourself or at a spoken word event.

    ii. **Mapping Yesterday's Truths**
        1. Sketch a map of your community based on your memory
        2. Check out your neighborhood and mark off all the landmarks and points you got correct
        3. Reflect on ways you can improve your memory

3) **Group Discussion (if applicable)**
    i. What lies do you believe we continue to hold on to about history and how do we challenge those lies?

The Ablest Queen (c. 1500 B.C.)
The ability of nature can only be activated if you purposefully walk with it.

Due to my travels through time,
they crowned me as the greatest then.
As Hatshepsut, my mind
marched with swords into males' dens.
My eyes speared the hearts of males' egos.
They acknowledged me by my birth name:
"Khummit Amen Hatshepsitou"
– "Loving One", before a need to change too.

My Temple itself, golden,
woven in the fabrics of time.
Chief Architect Senmut,
what a mind?
Golden black as I.
My temple, a world of its own
unlatching everyone's windows
obliging the sun to gleam from this throne.

A royal sight of things,
Empress, majesty.
I was Queen, but a (King) in disguise.
Bestowed years like a God, a sculptor,
whom shaped the *lands I conquered,*
poured music into *hearts as a vivifier,*
as a gold-adorned skyscraper
whom reflected the title "Mighty One".

My ethereal form incarnated in Southern Egypt
where family links a complex path to Sudan,
Grandma Nefertari-Aahmes of Ethiopia
among others is how it all began.
No King will ever,
try as he might,
overtake my legacy
once history gets it right.

1) **Reflection Actions**
    i. **History's Gems and Pretenses**
        1. What does it mean to walk with nature or walk with history?
        2. Have you pretended to be anything before? How did you decide to no longer pretend?
2) **Creative Activities**
    i. **Sculpting History**
        1. Try your hand at sculpting; get a sculpting set with clay
        2. Sculpt your favorite figure or item from history
        3. Display it somewhere in your home as your own decorations

    ii. **Growing with Nature**
        1. Check on your plant, remember to water it today, and speak with it about the new things you are learning about yourself and this poetry book
3) **Group Discussion (if applicable)**
    i. How does Hatshepsut remind you of some of the things that are happening in history?
    ii. How might her legacy be valuable for many to learn about today?

Animal Love
To love beyond one's own level is the ultimate compassion.

Shadow or Shawlo rolled off my tongue; his name.
Fluffy hair, bright eyes, a best friend
jumping like a cricket in joy; a loving game.
Laying on his last bed, his memories remained
as they torpedoed to the heavens
mailing a child a memory stamped
in mind showing Shadow's fame.

Then,
Jacob and Esther, stealthy climbers
agile in the game of quietude.
Our small space, a
    box
for ours and their room
did not matter to them with food.
Droppings anywhere and everywhere
colored mother's eyes with a red mood.

Then news of America came
through phone lines;
then news of a time
to giveaway.
The tears then ran down the cheeks
of a little child letting go of childhood glee.

1) **Reflection Actions**
    i. **Love and Furry Companions**
        1. What is compassion to you and how do you show it to others? If you have a pet, how has it shown you compassion?

2) **Creative Activities**
    i. **Time Spent**
        1. Spend time researching about a favorite animal, what it symbolizes and how it might relate to who you are
    ii. **Early Morning Stroll**
        1. Go to the park one early morning
        2. As you stroll, jot down the sensations you feel, the sounds you hear, and the animals those sounds come from.
        3. Reflect on the interconnection between the animals and nature

3) **Group Discussion (if applicable)**
    i. Are dogs the only animals that are man's best friend or are there others?
    ii. Which animal is best to keep as a pet? Why?

Foreign Mi Guh

Teach the foundation for a child's growth and new experiences will multiply through exploration.

A Wite people alone mi tink mi did ago see.
A young mind fimi seem to be.
When mi step off a deh plane
mi yeye dem widened to deh *apple-like* city.
When mi glance back,
yuh cyaan hear whole 'eap a laafta mi get wid pity.

Mi did tink a dem kindness like seh mi a Martin.
Mi did question dem badness like seh mi a Malcolm
and get stuck inna deh miggle willfully.
Mi did hear seh Baldwin find deh miggle silly.

Cause a dat,
wah likkle mind did shoot up inna deh sky.
Nat even deh sun coulda bun mi curious eyes.
Garvey did seh freedom
nah guh com from closin deh blinds.
An a past full wid years
like wah full cup,
just did a ask fi be drunk up,
but don't get drunk up
pon deh histery,
cause it easy fi get lost.

Suh den mi get inna wah shifting zone,
weh mi did waa deh past a mi home.
How easy it coulda be
if mi did fly back wid glee.
Or maybe, weh mi did see

anno weh mi did waa encounta fi real.
Eitha way, whe-eva mi ya guh,

mi we memba weh mi a come from.

Cause a yute just waah get food
from deh peace yim a luk
from in a *deh world's history bed.*

1) **Reflection Actions**
    i. **Exploration Through Naivety**
        1. How have you pushed beyond your ignorance to make transformations in your life?

2) **Creative Activities**
    i. **Becoming**
        1. Thinking about a "seed,", draw what its transformation would look like when it becomes a plant. Name that plant.
        2. Considering the image for this poem and the title which translates to "Foreign I went", draw an image of your own in five minutes that responds to the poem.

3) **Group Discussion (if applicable)**
    i. Why is it important to remember where we are coming from?
    ii. Can being naïve have its benefits or is it a dangerous thing?

Sculpted Years: Yaad Memories
Culmination is the act for a new start.

From the place of "Irie Vibes", "Ya Mon",
"Likkle Moor" and "Wha Gwan,"
the "Land of Wood and Wata",
paints of gold, green, yellow,
murals of Caribbean fellows,
                            sky bridge,
"In God We Trust"
stamped on blue, white, and red,
where history is fed,
thus fillings with more *arms*.

Perceptions of my decisions,
burst bubble, truths no longer forgone
while I constructed questions of reality
even when I fell short
of untangling the ironies of a place with all sorts
of confusing battles with minds of all forms.

There are those who wear red noses
with red afros
wanting to get acceptance
– from *caged* sparrows –
Kids wanna be ^{eagles in the sky}
                  Young Royals to Pharaohs.
                       Fledglings wanna fly
                          to the sky with bows and arrows;
but lack nourishing sessions to healing,
answers to questions aren't easily revealing.

Is it caused by leaders:
pots without food for thought?
What's a thought
if it wasn't caught?
Can't be caught cause of *party* living?
Little nature skimming
of *nature's* feelings?
Shutting eyes to system drillings
equal empty barrels thinking?

When I was young,
empty barrels made the most noise.
My eyes glued onto childhood toys:
Turtle Hermit,
my friends and I practiced Ki – poise.
It was a little world,
we were little boys.
I liked grandma's spicy strong soup
with dumplings. Bugs, Daffy, the Rangers
were all lumped in.
Shadow growls, Jacob and Esther prowl
then a plane was the bridge for moving
to *Adult* house *Swimming* loud,
it was a secret with no approving.

That was life as I began turning.
Mixing flavors, thirteen I was consuming
NEWS shaping pains
into a wretched world devolving
with triggers ticking, thundering, traveling.

Bang!
Big screens stuffing sin into a high school kid.
In class, unaware of red and blue (h)arming pills.
Reading made me better at schooling quiz.
Same quiz for all – currency bid.
We were currency kids.

Kids, the yutes
from deh time of popular games
bac in games room.
Tryin' to throw down our presence
like we were the main goons.
Paintin' an image of the main moon,
so *Curby* was game too.
The magnificence
of the (in)sane moon,
as if in the fame room.
Excited fingers on buttons
brought shivers from wind killas,
they were the playas
garnered audiences as room fillas.
Scene for museum thrillas.
Later I drew like the artist wielda.
Filled your minds with artist glimma,
you reflected, mutated into parts of me;
an artist hitta. Inspired minds like the artist thrilla,
painted a spark emitta.

1) **Reflection Actions**
    i. **Childhood Memories: A Seed becomes a plant**
        1. "Think about your accolades and actions that led you to this point in your life. How have you shown appreciation and/or gratitude to the people who have helped you in that process?
        2. How are the lessons and experiences you've had supporting your journey today?

2) **Creative Activities**
    i. **Open the "Letter to Young You"**
        1. Add any other experiences you want to add to the letter as you think about how this poem is a sculpture of this book.
        2. Put the letter away again and reopen it after the last poem in the last book and complete the activity for the poem then.

3) **Group Discussion (if applicable)**
    i. The impact of media and technology on young people's perceptions of the world. How do you think this influences their aspirations and realities?

The Journey Continues in the next book of poetry

"World Reflections"

Thank you for reading and taking action, Stay Tuned!

www.ingramcontent.com/pod-product-compliance
Lightning Source LLC
Chambersburg PA
CBHW041216070526
44583CB00001B/7